Heavenly Father's Great Plan For Me!

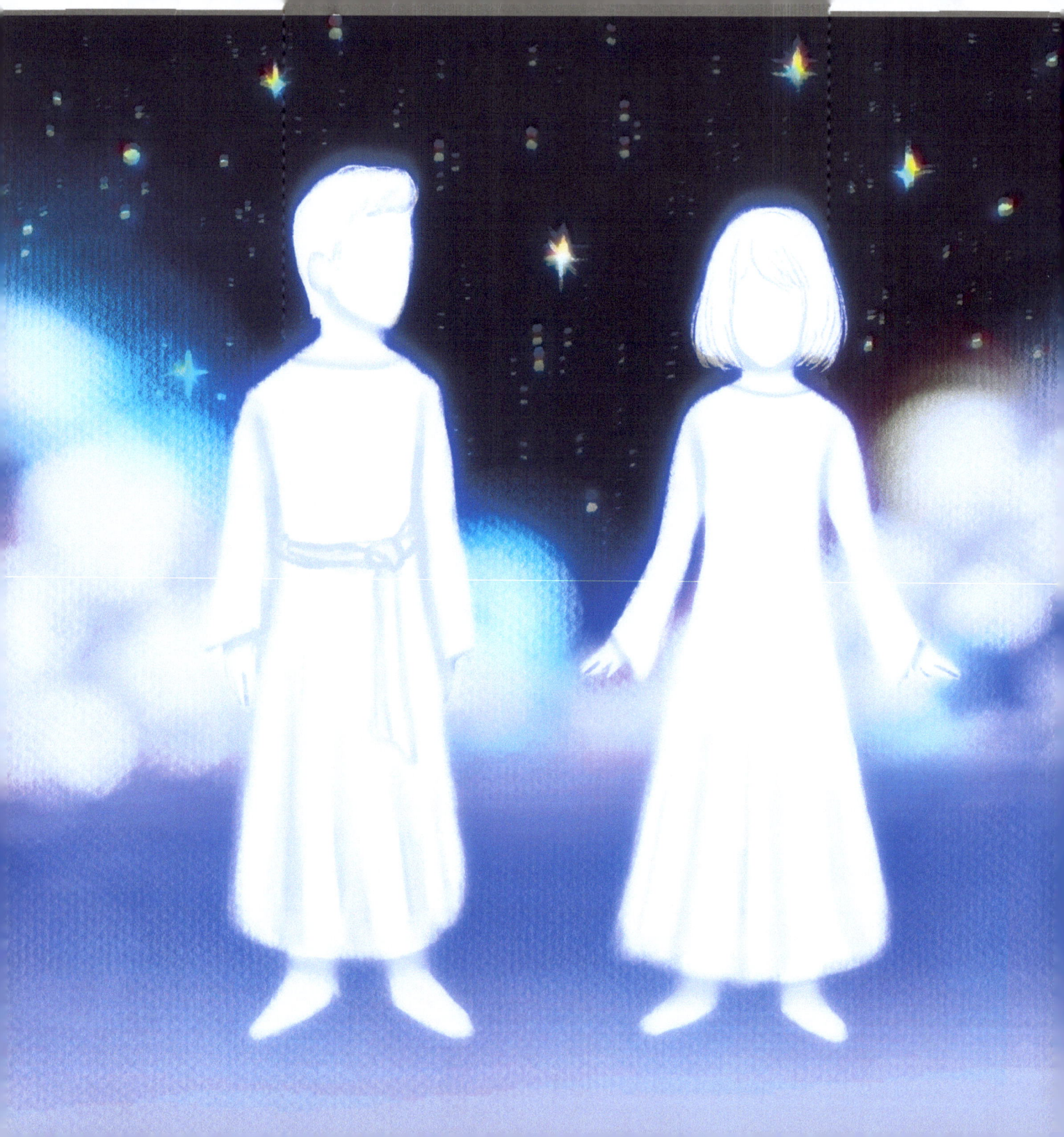

A long time ago, our spirits lived in Heaven with Heavenly Father and Jesus.

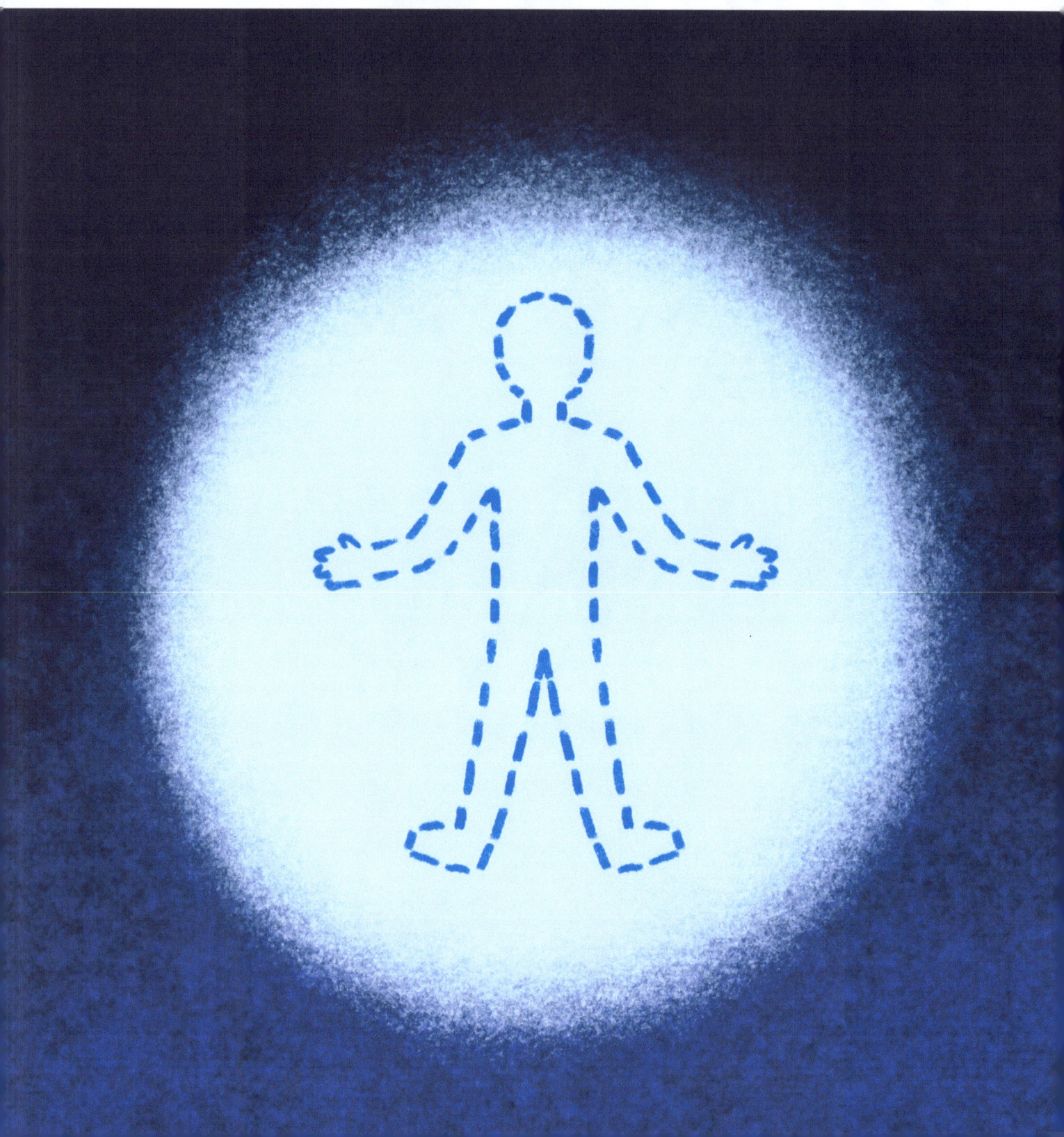

We didn't have bodies like He does. So, Heavenly Father created a plan so we could have one.

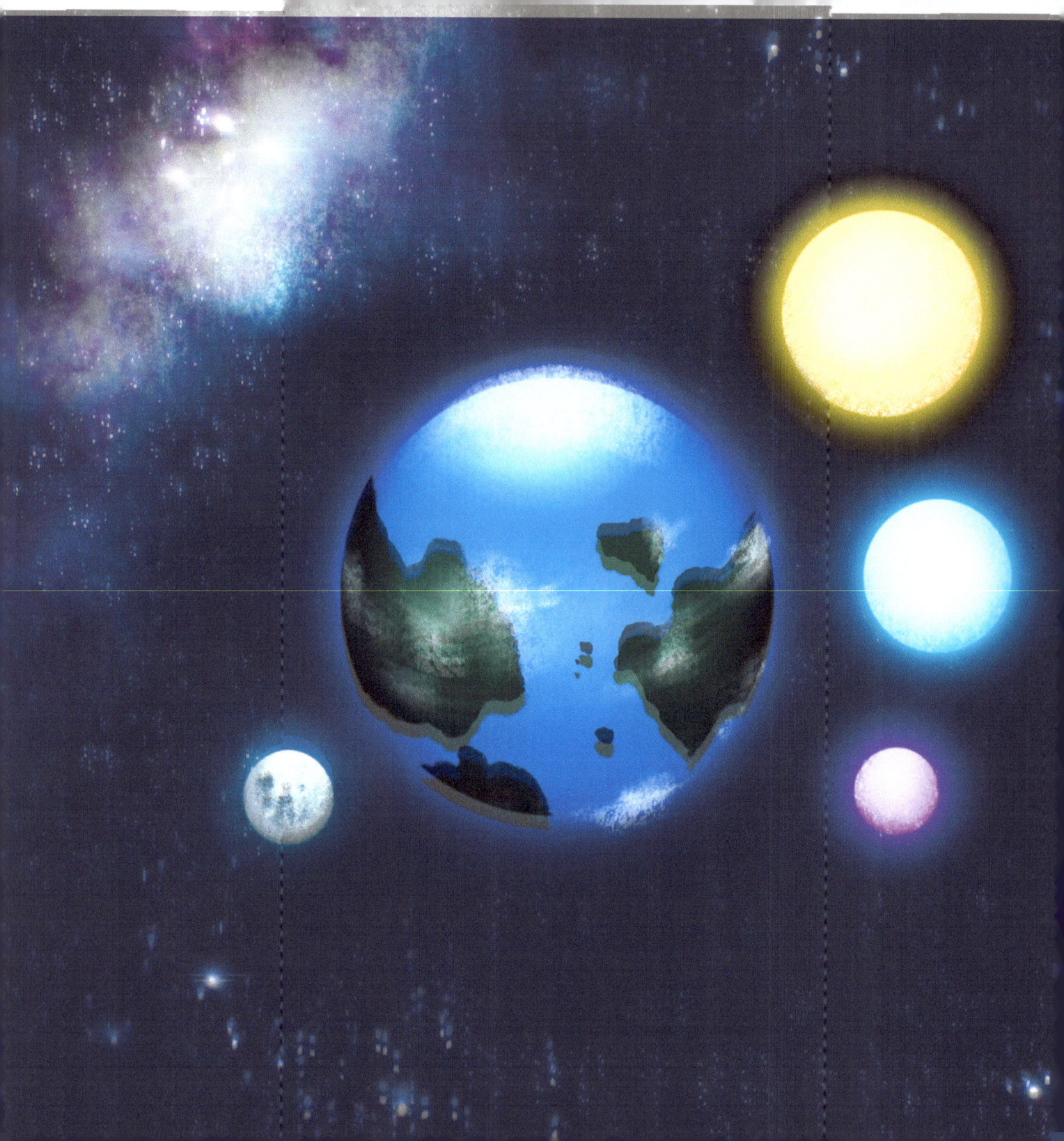

He called it "the great plan of happiness!"

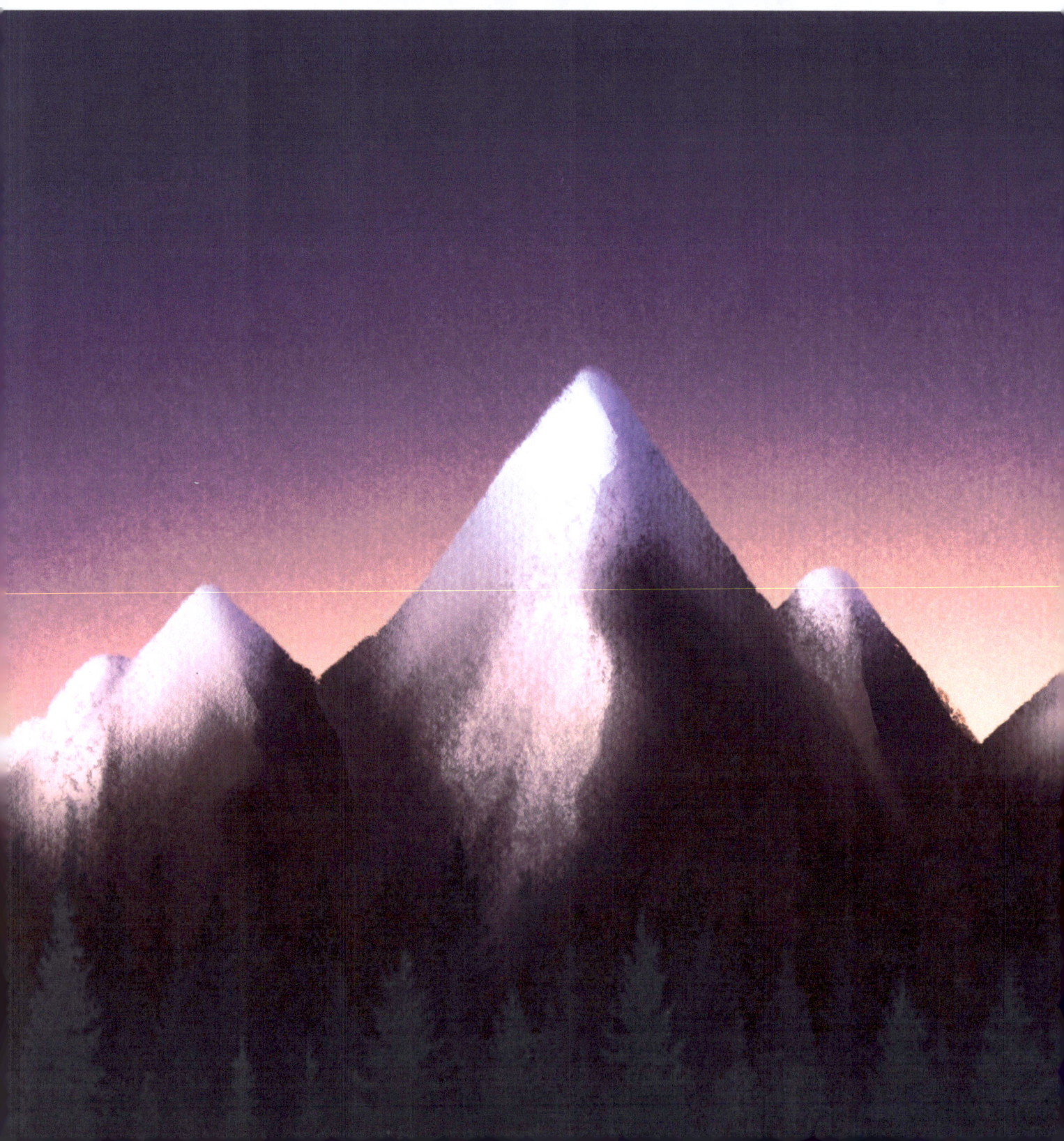

Heavenly Father and Jesus created a beautiful world for us to live in.

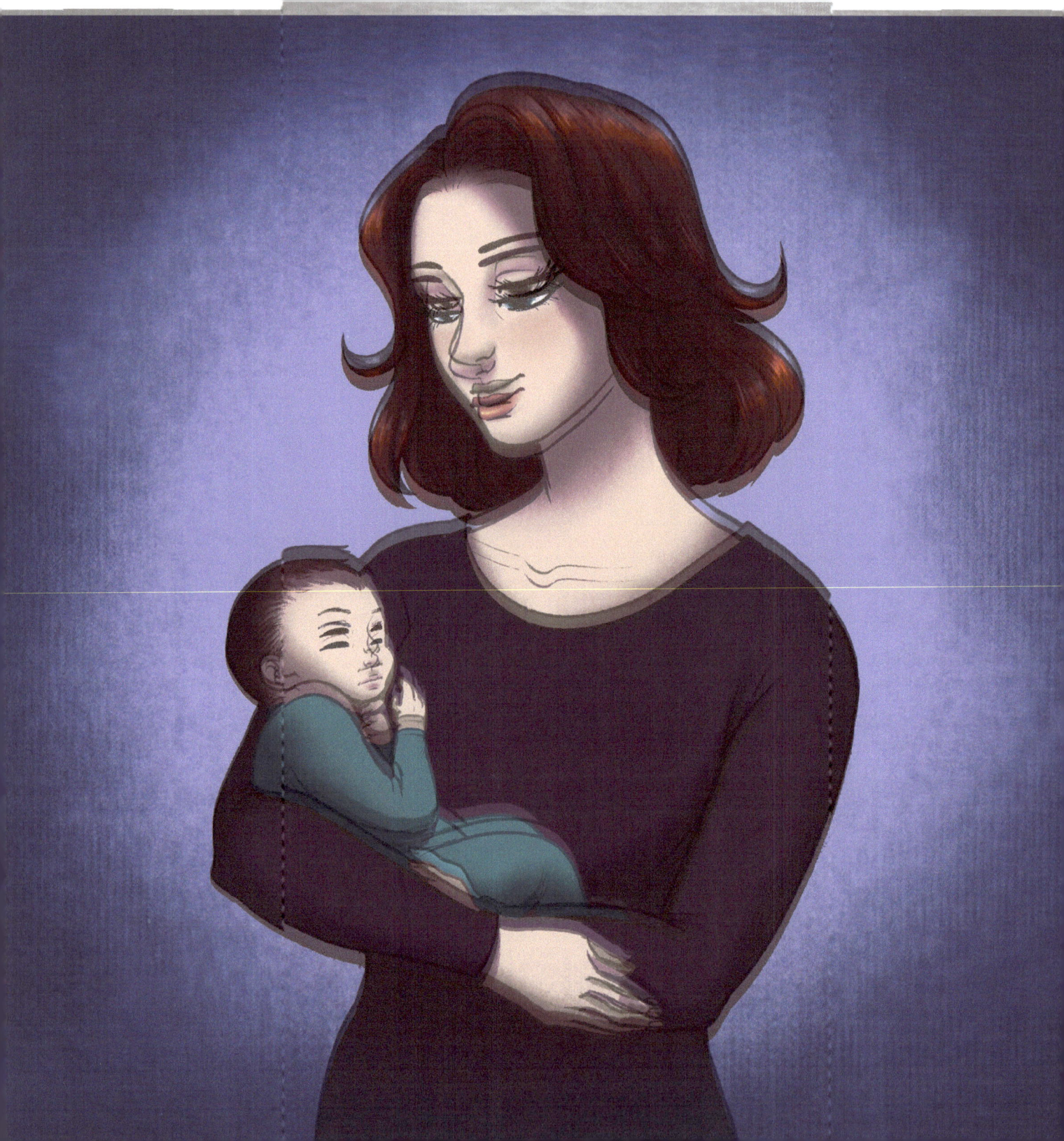

When we are born, we forget about how we lived with Heavenly Father, so that we can learn and make choices.

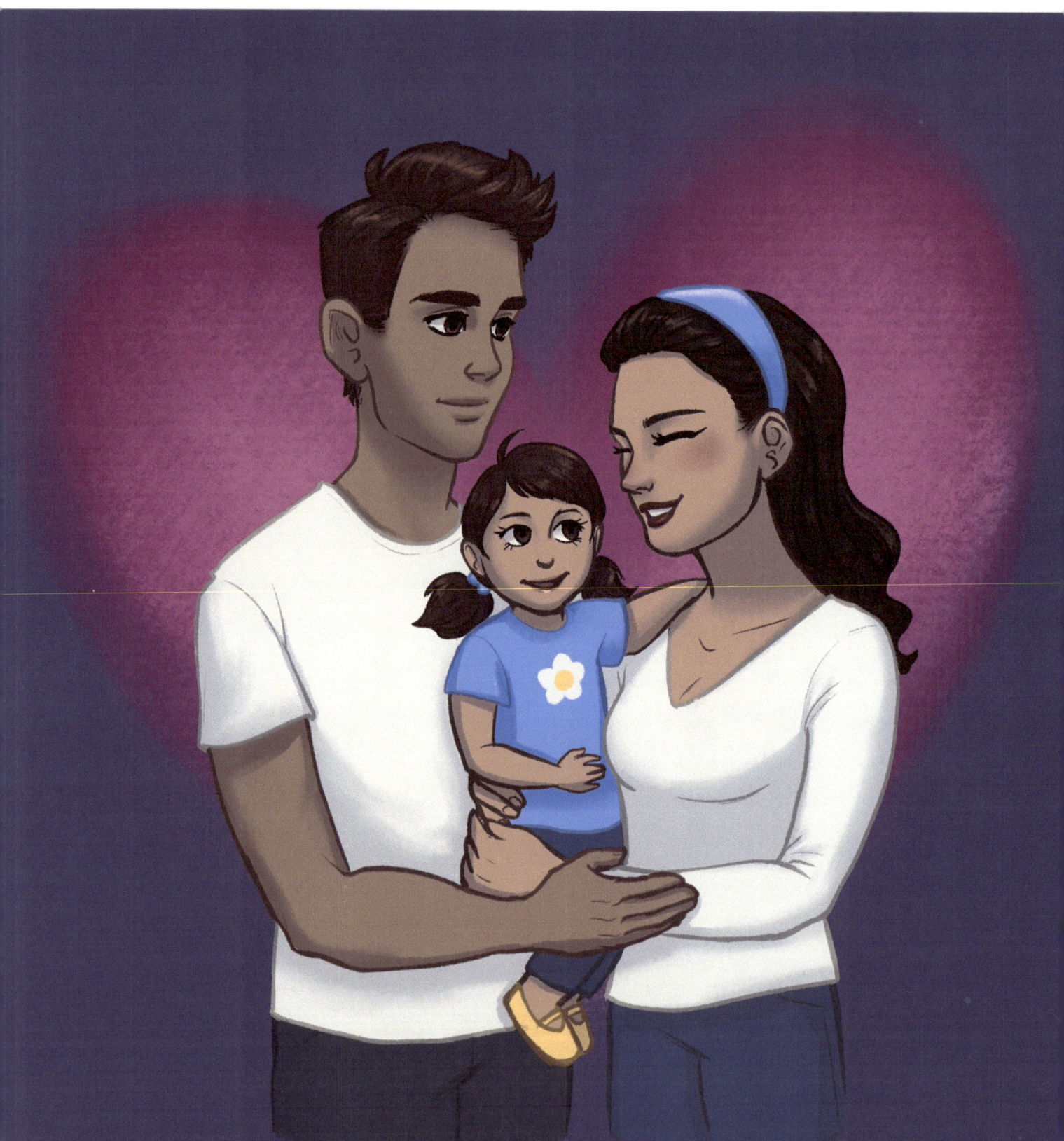

On Earth we are born into families who love us, teach us, and protect us.
They can help us know how to choose the right!

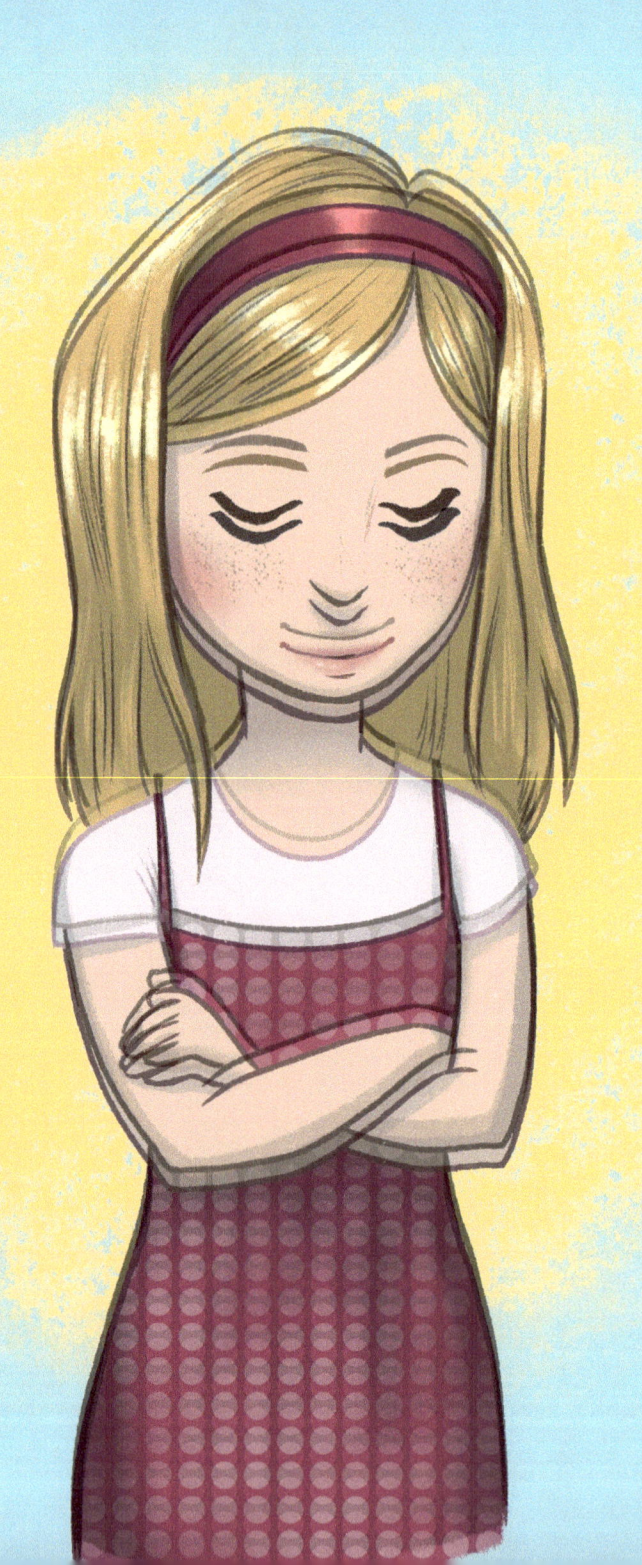

Even though we live far from Heavenly Father, He is always there to help us if we pray and ask for His help.

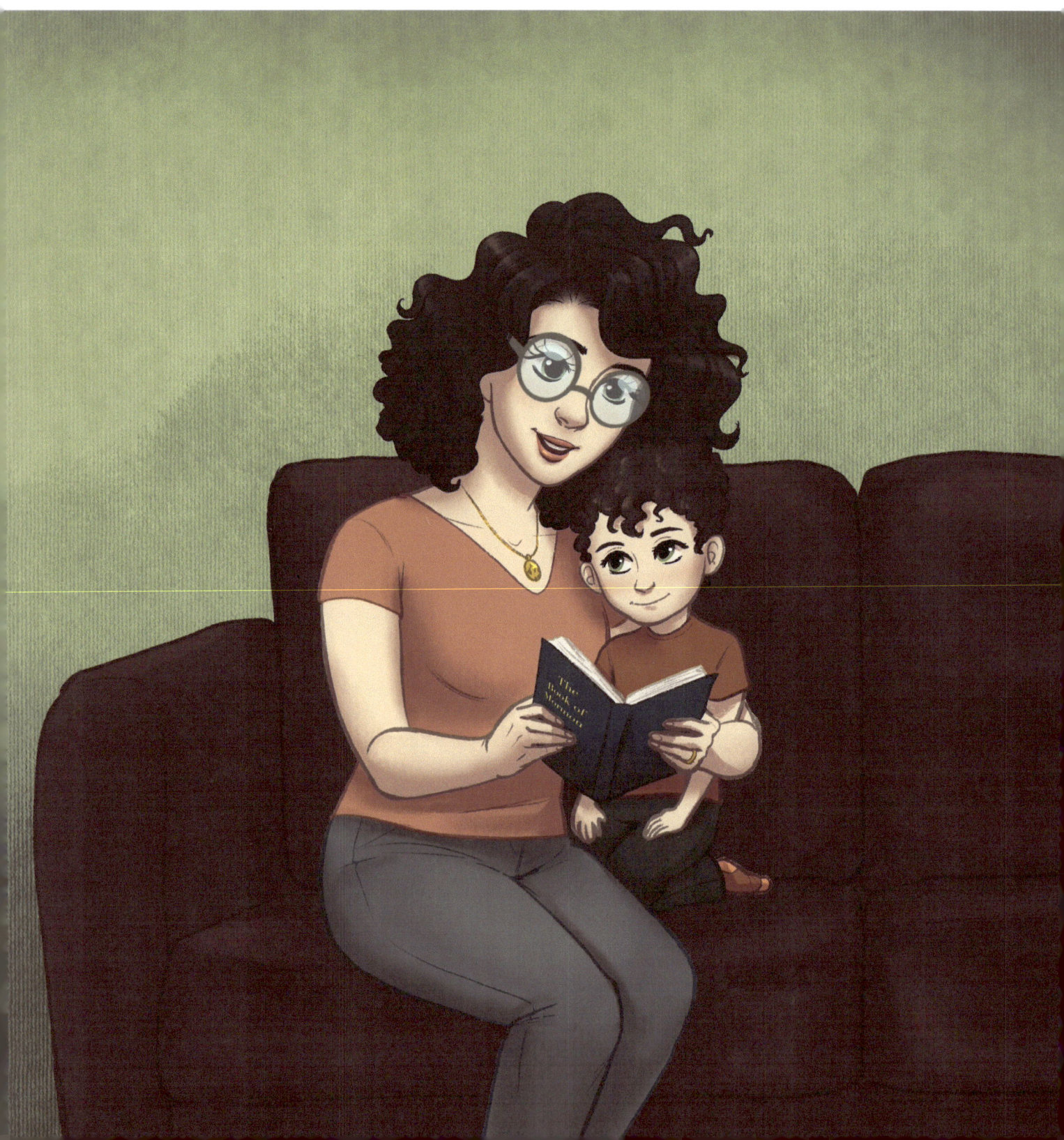

Our parents should help teach us how Heavenly Father wants us to live.

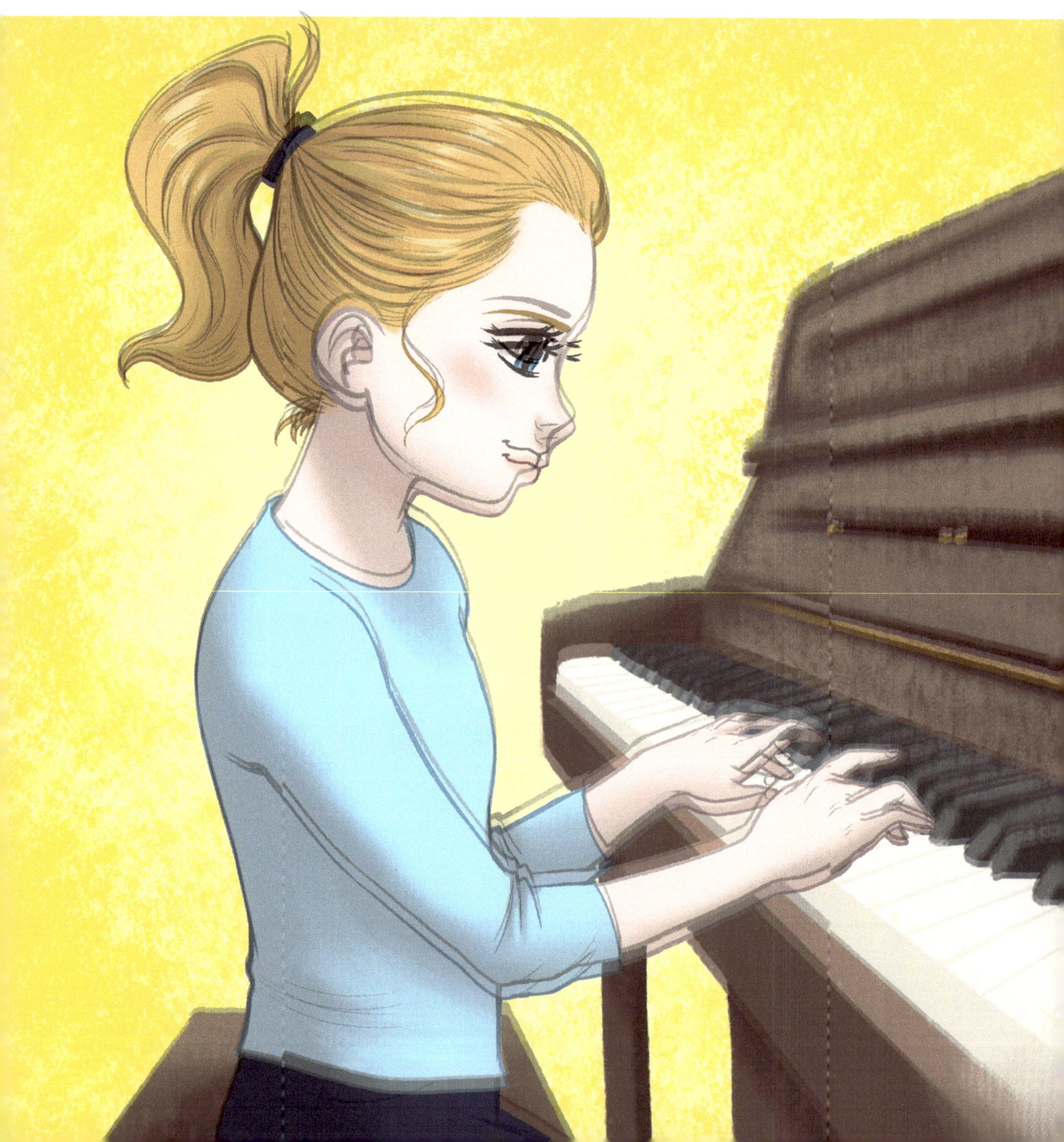

When we grow up we learn through experience. Heavenly Father wants our minds to grow In knowledge, and our bodies to grow in strength.

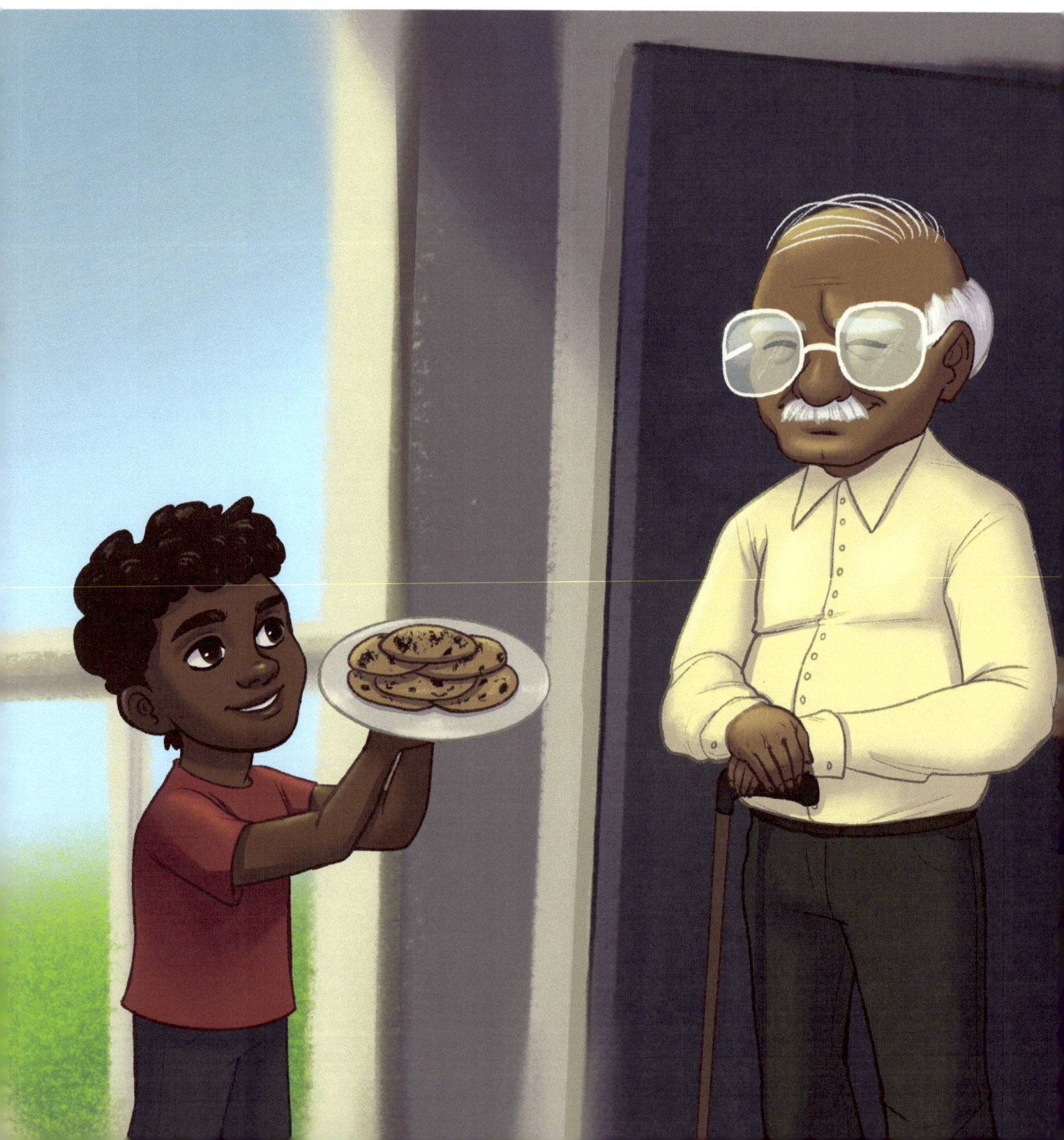

We learn how to make friends, serve our neighbors, and love our families.

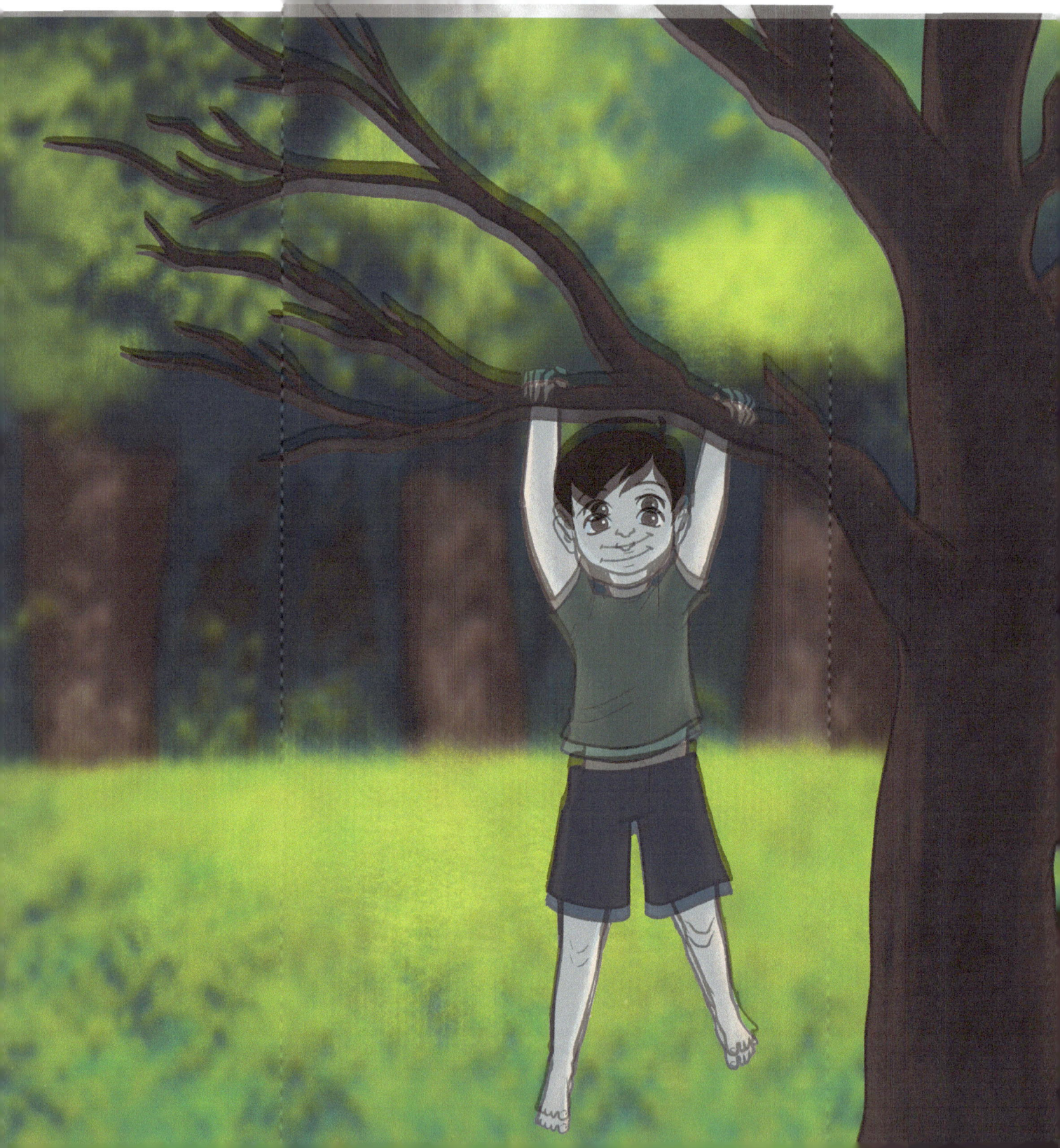

We learn how to do fun things like run, swim and climb.

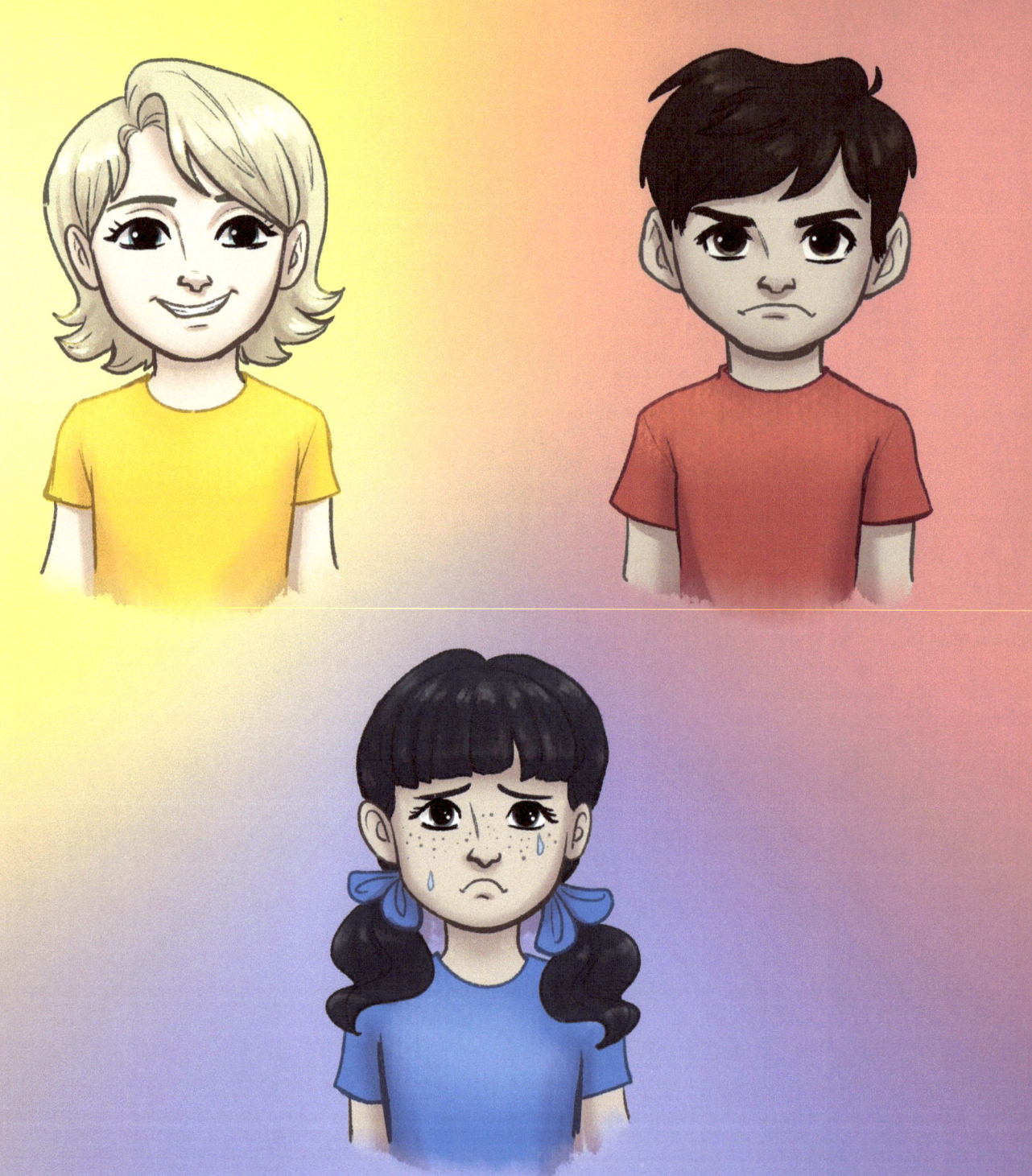

We learn about our feelings and how to understand them.

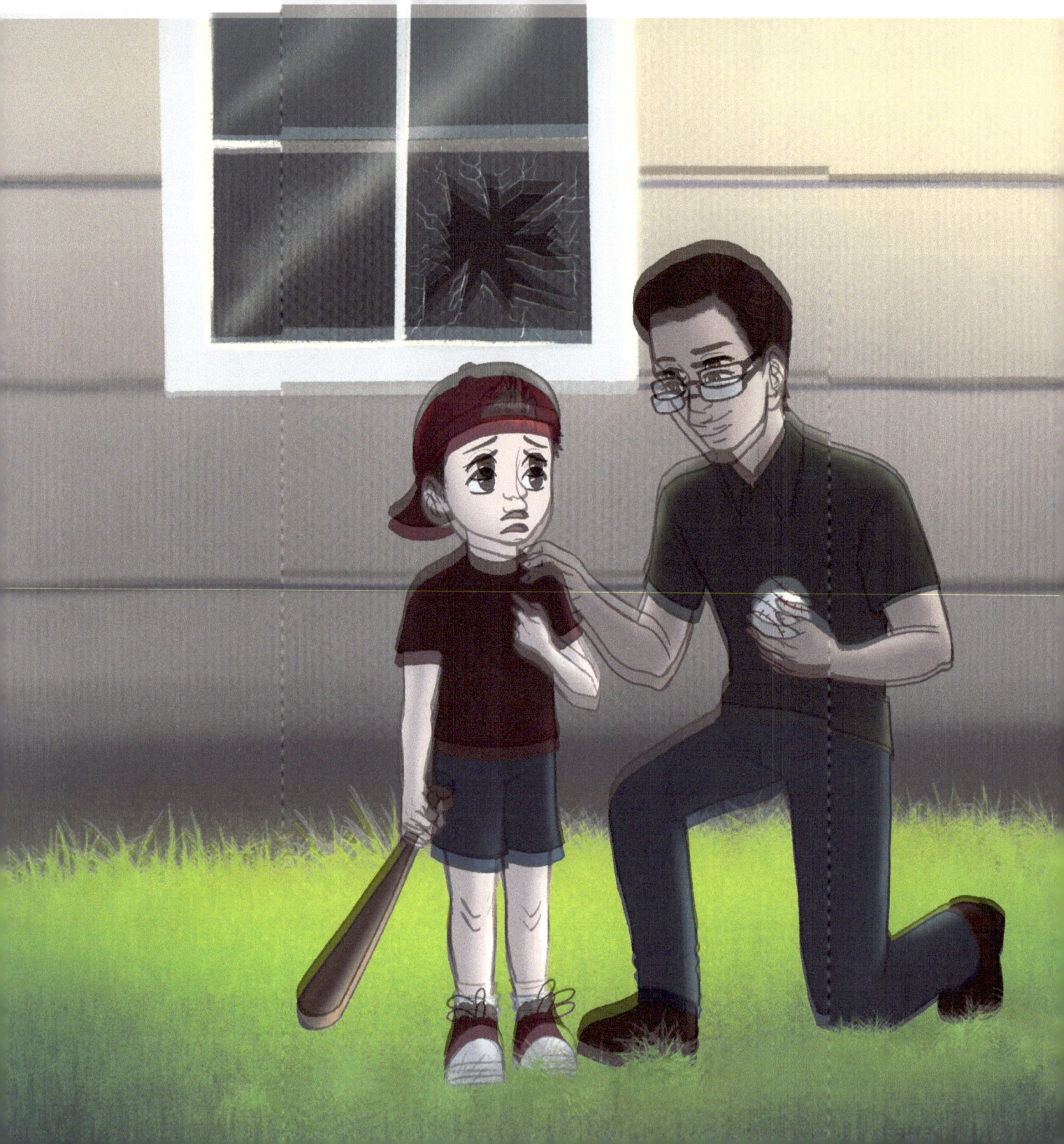

We learn right from wrong,
and we learn how to choose
the right.

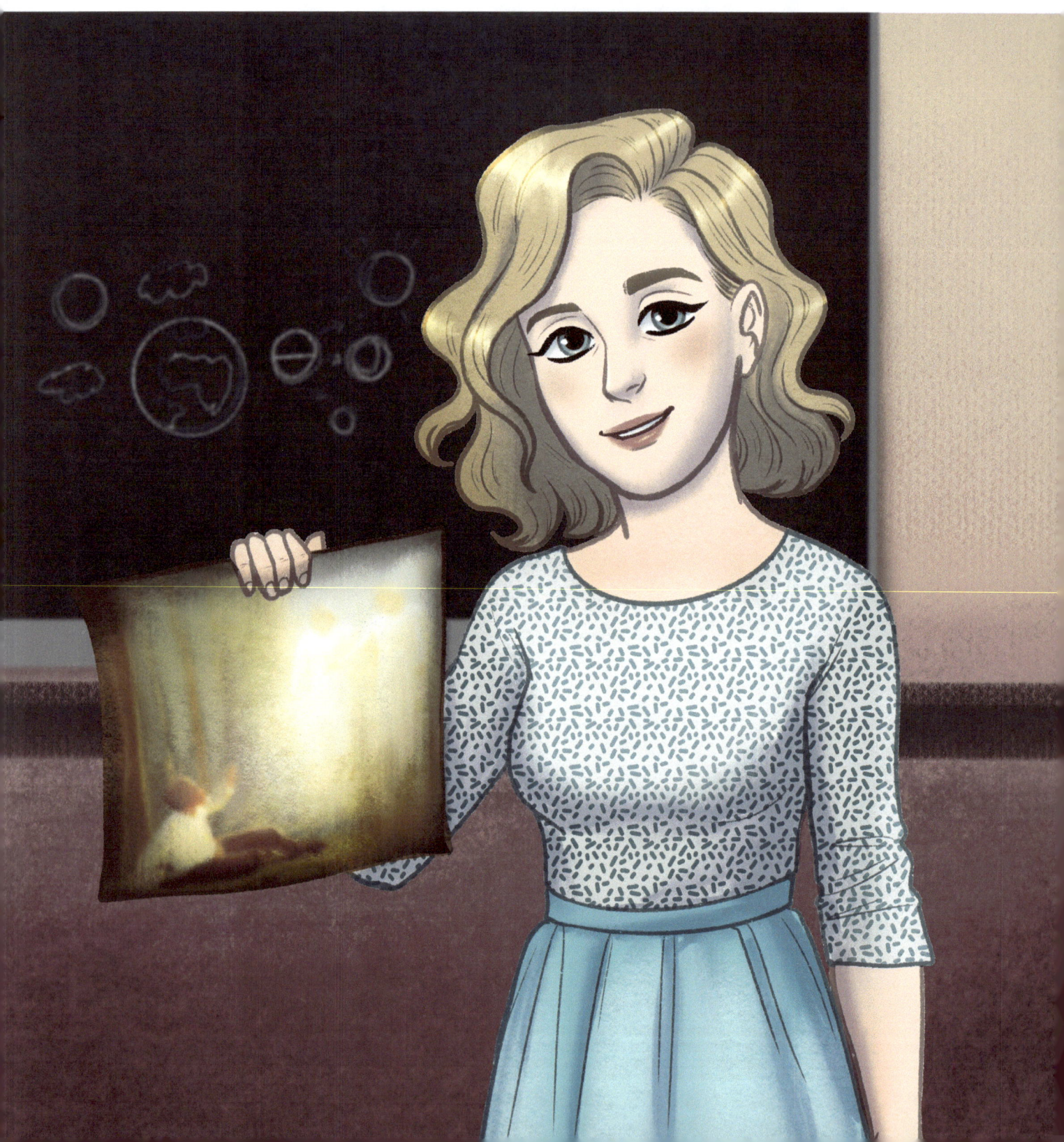

We learn about Heavenly Father and Jesus at church.

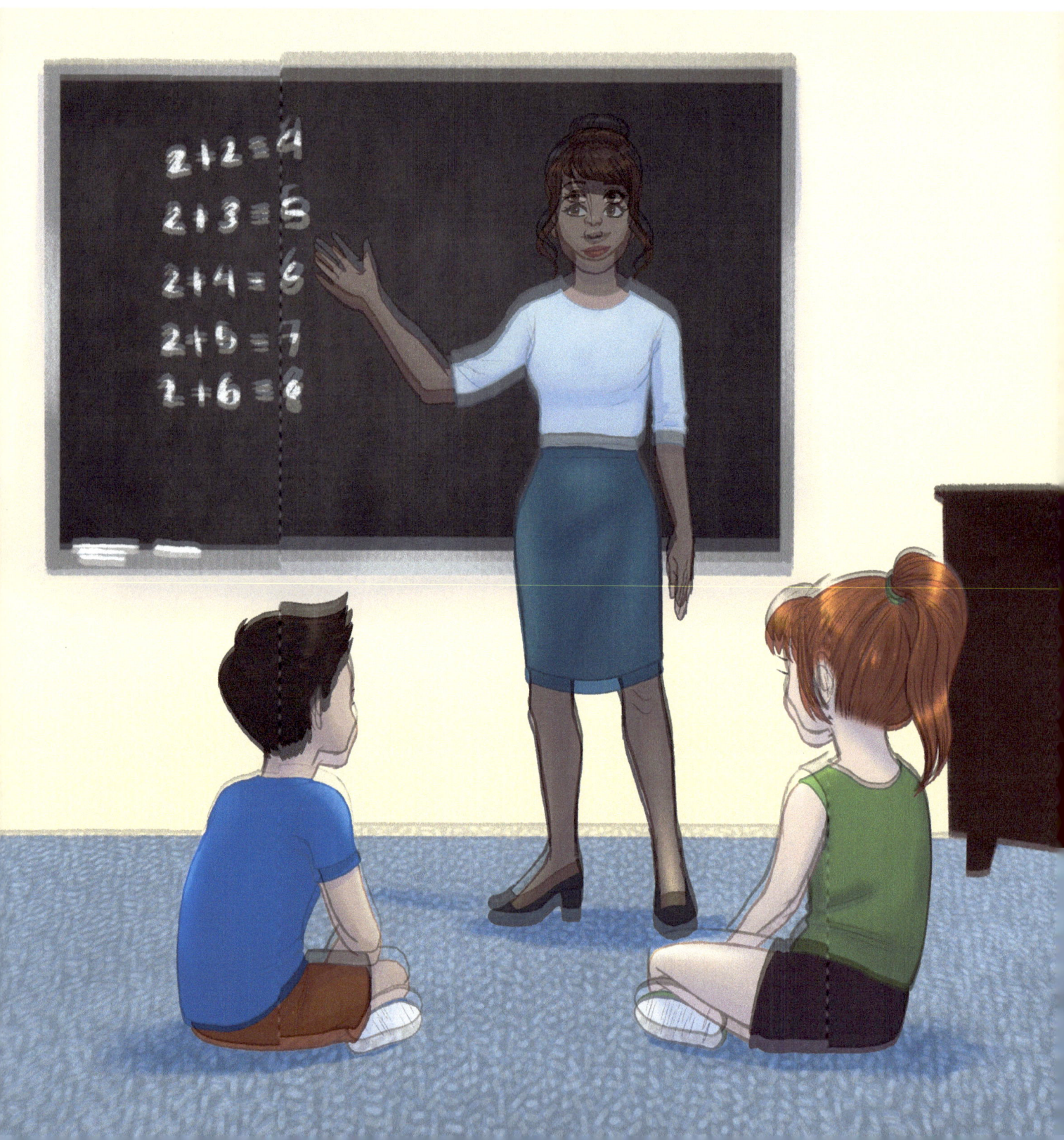

and we learn about the world at school.

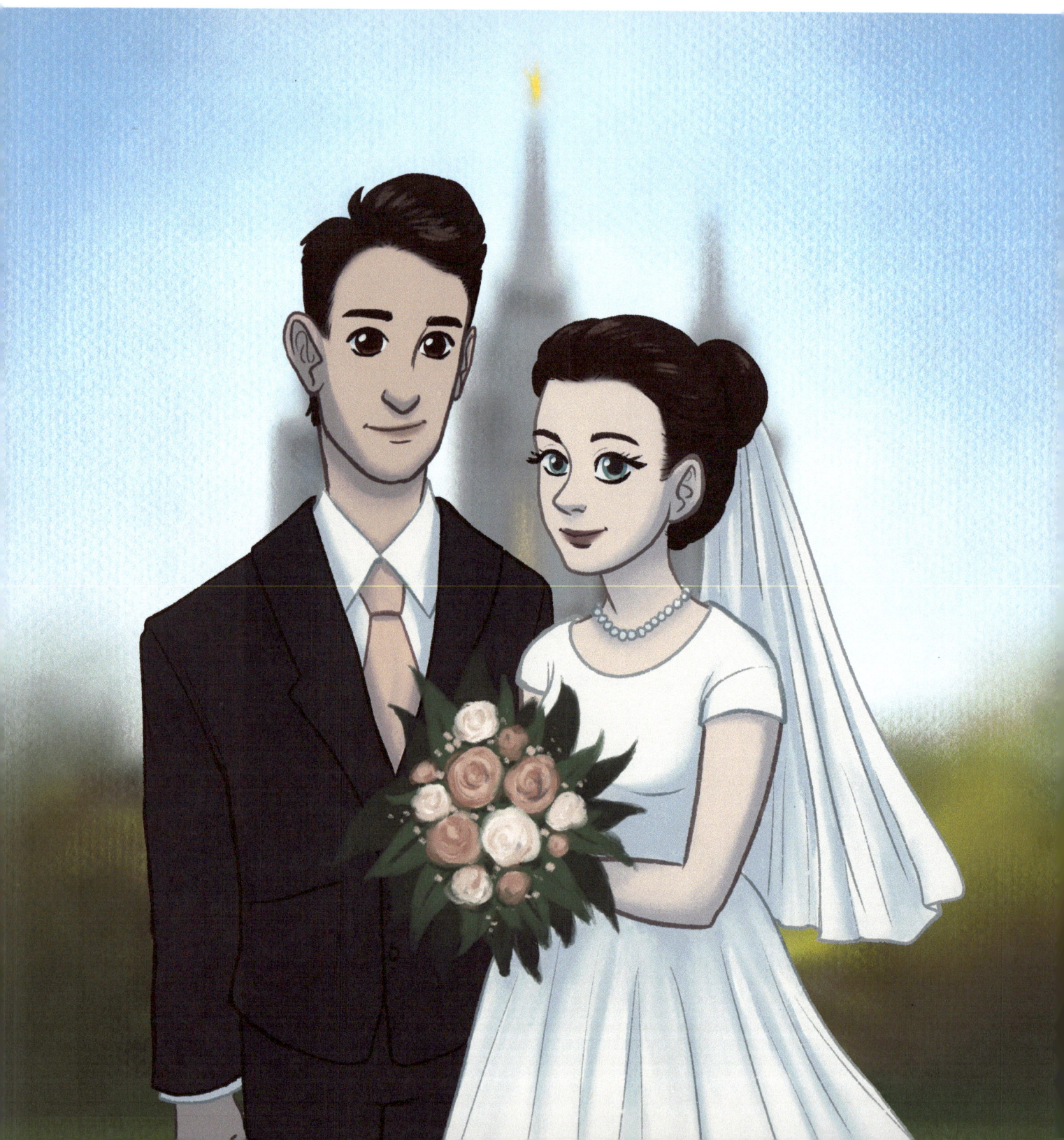

One day you can get married in the temple! We have the chance to become Mothers and Fathers, and have our own families to love and teach.

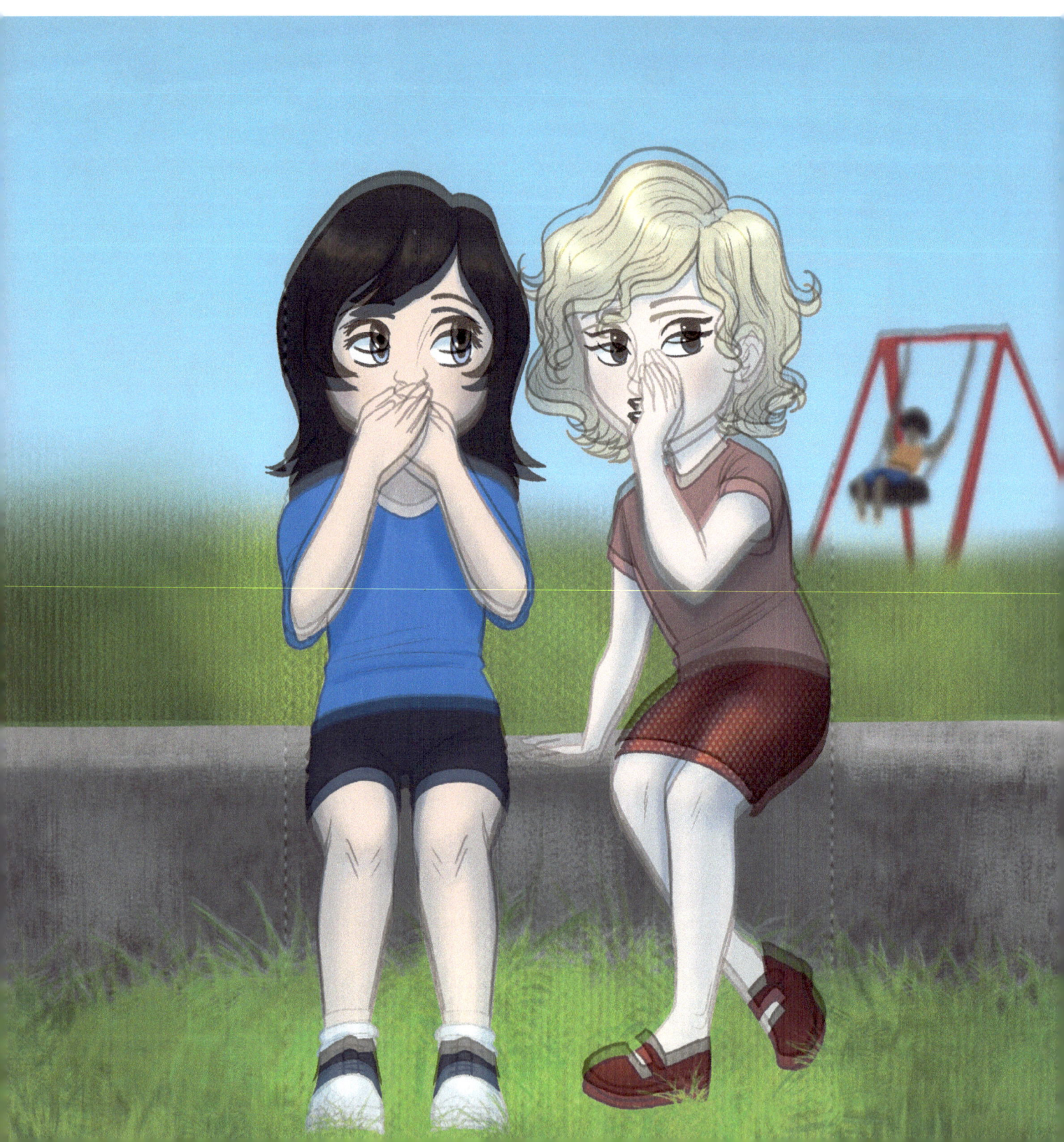

Another thing we learn about is that we make mistakes. Sometimes we do or say bad things. But that is part of life.

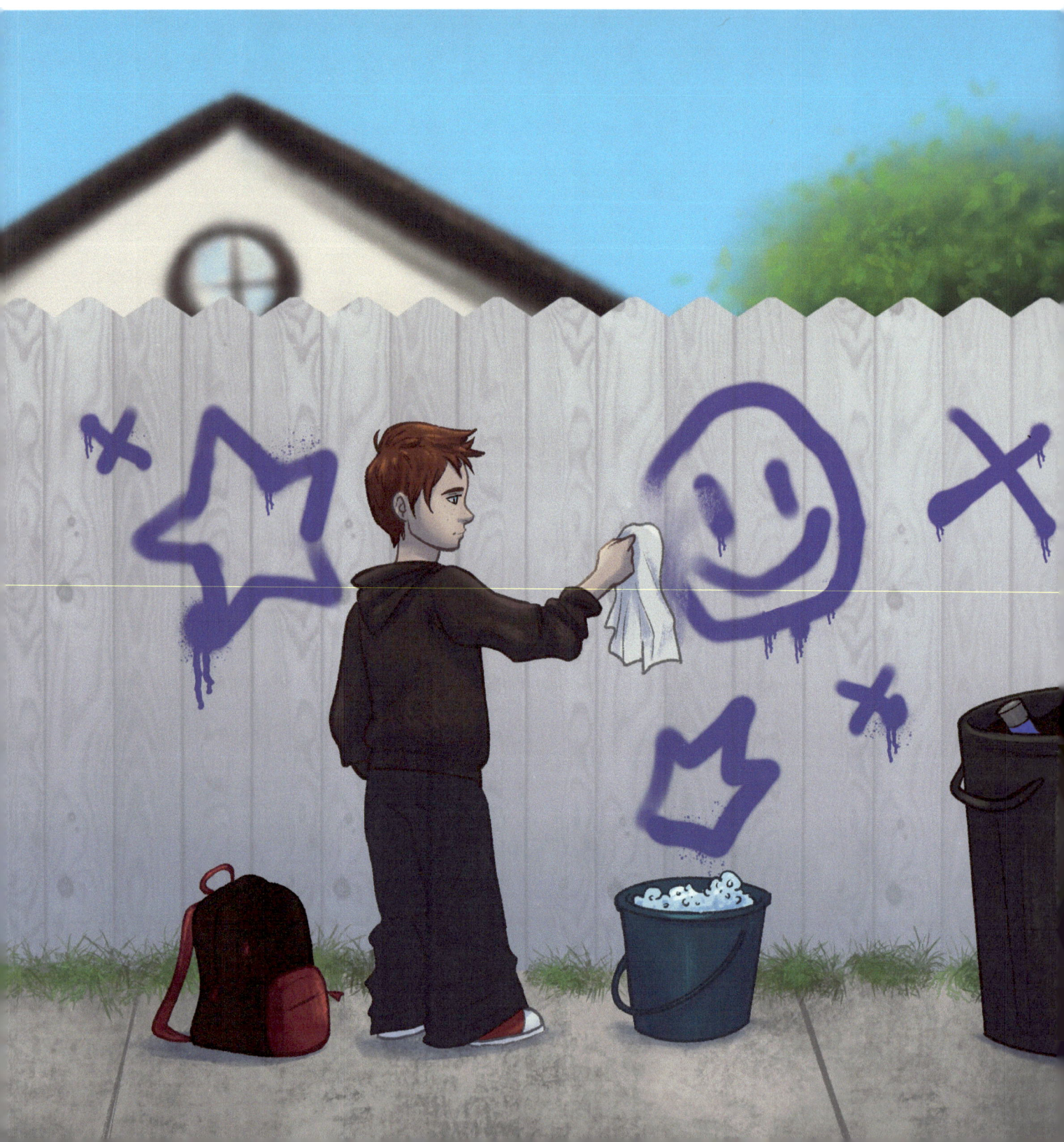

When we make mistakes, it makes Heavenly Father sad. But he loves us anyway, and wants us to have a chance to try again.

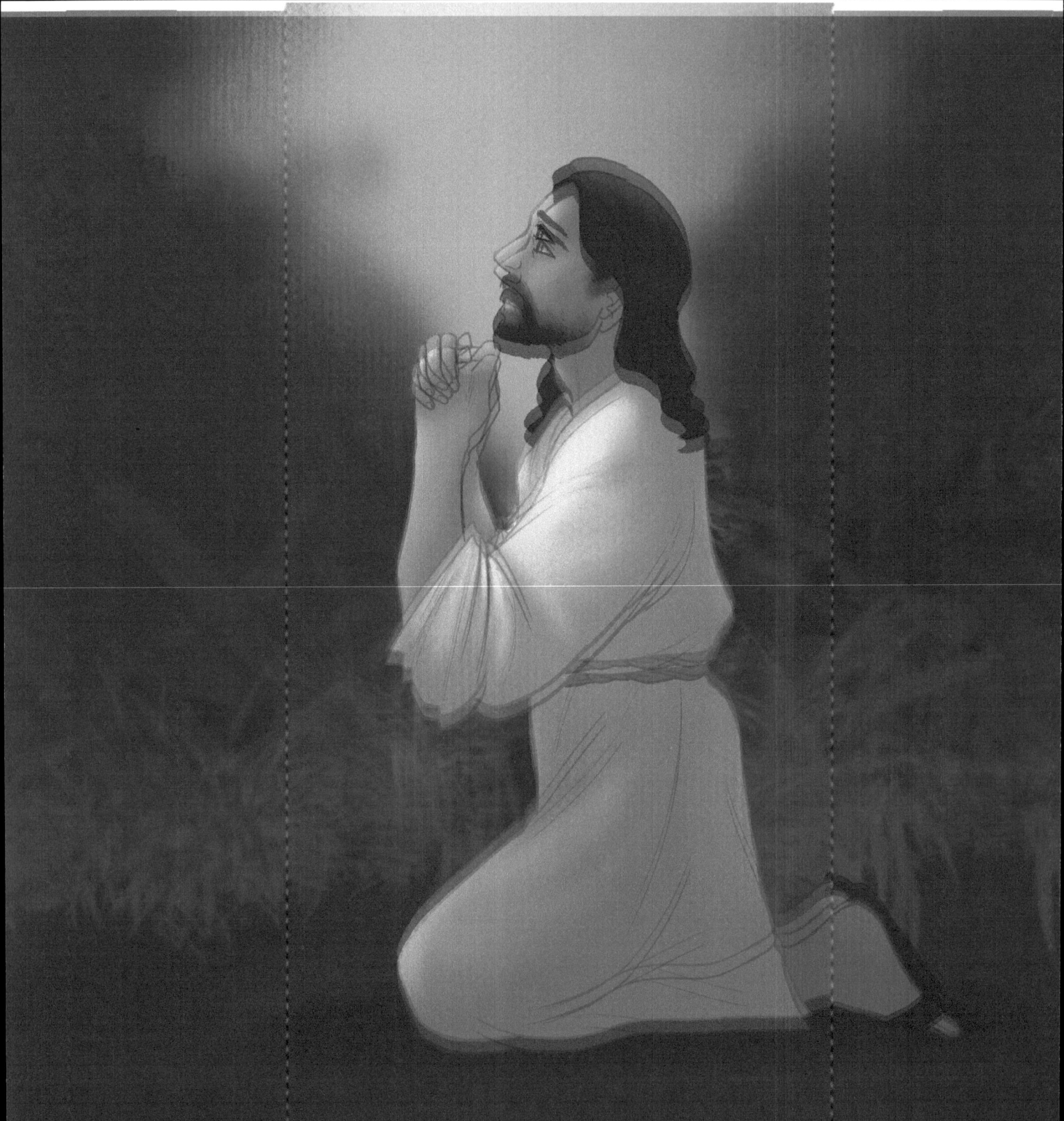

Jesus gave us a chance to try again when He died for us. Because of His sacrifice, we can say sorry to Heavenly Father, and try to be better.

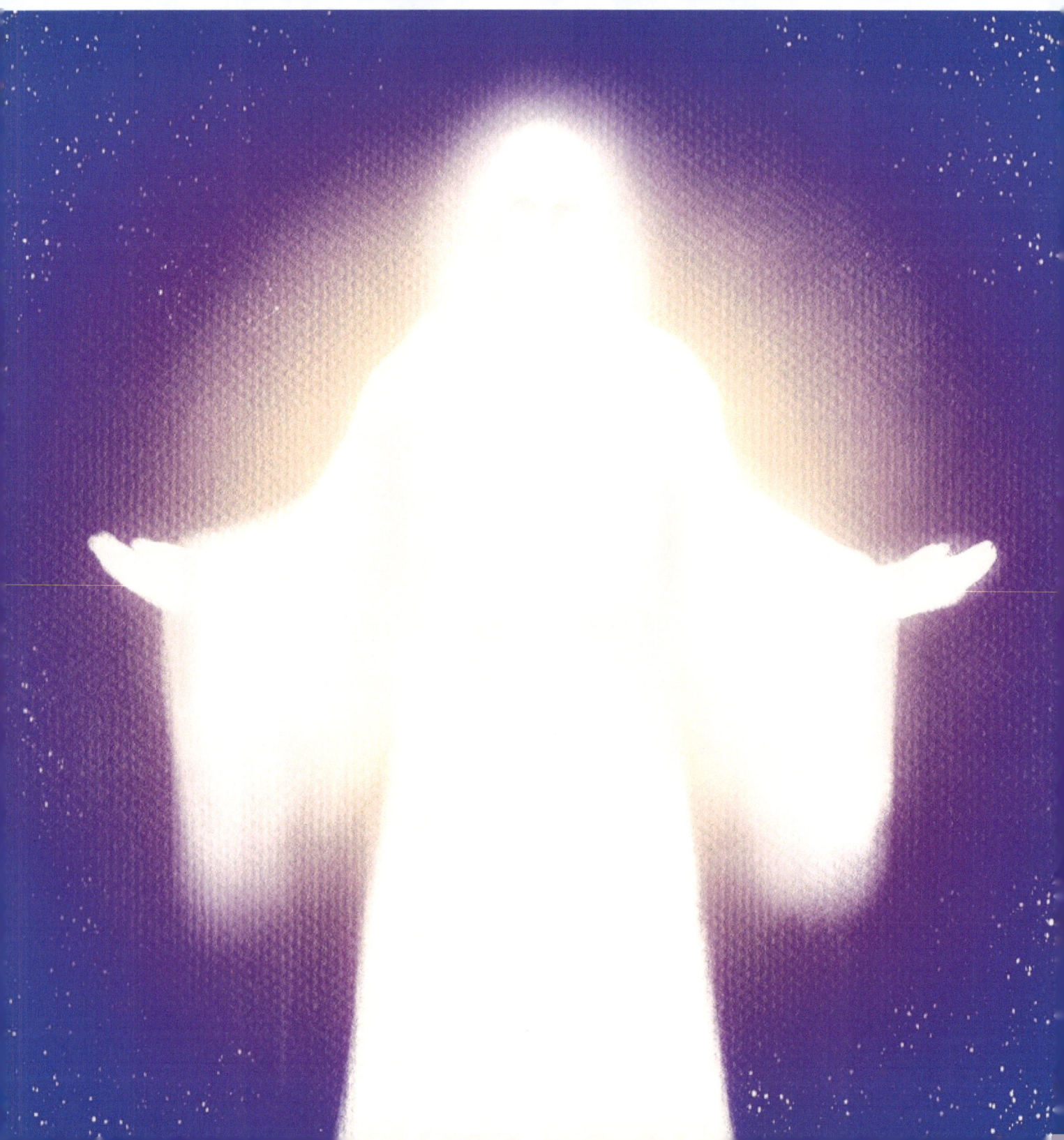

Heavenly Father is the Father of our spirits, so He loves us. He wants to forgive us. We can always talk to when we need Him.

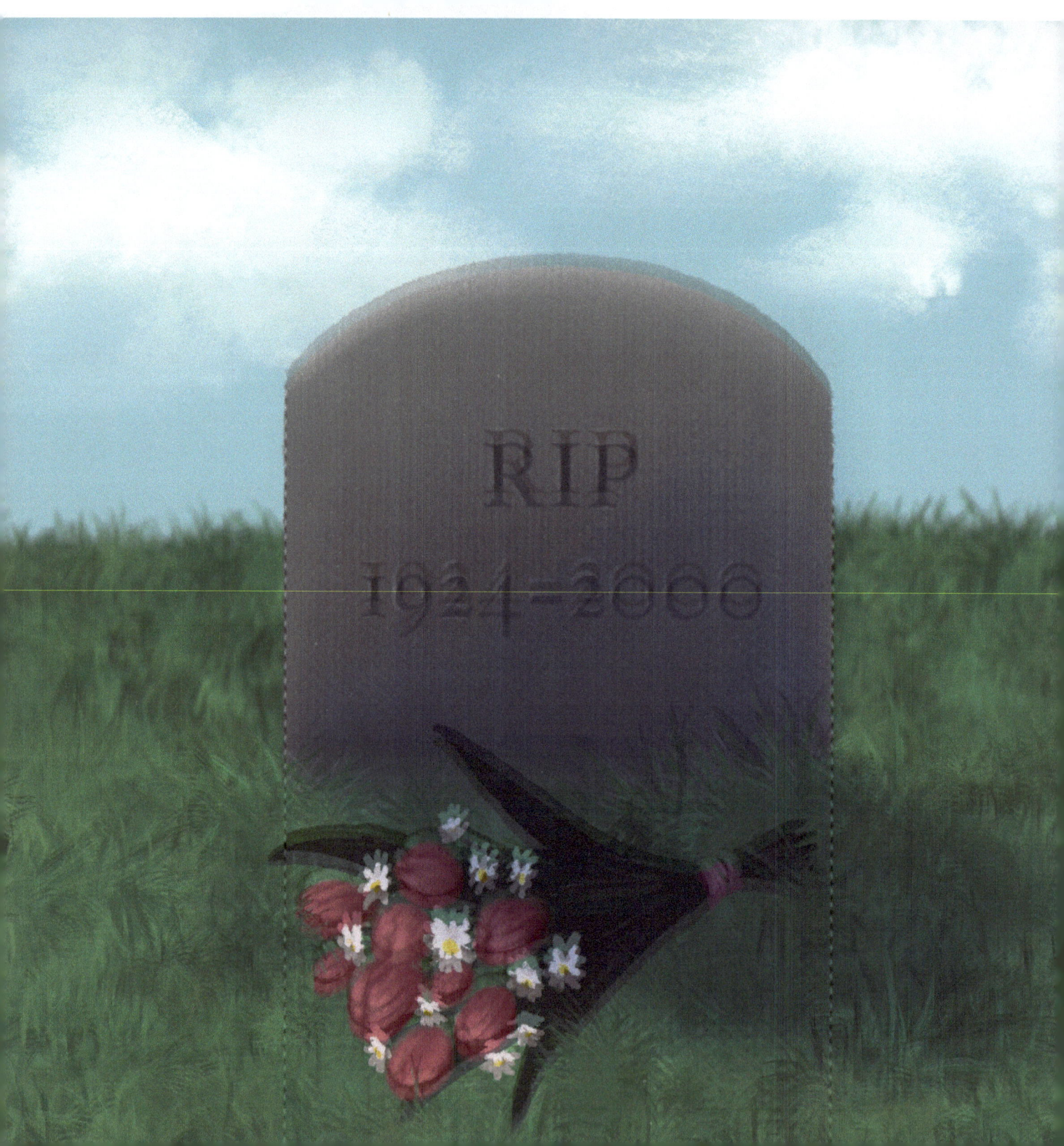

After many years on Earth, we eventually die, and our spirit goes to live with Heavenly Father again.

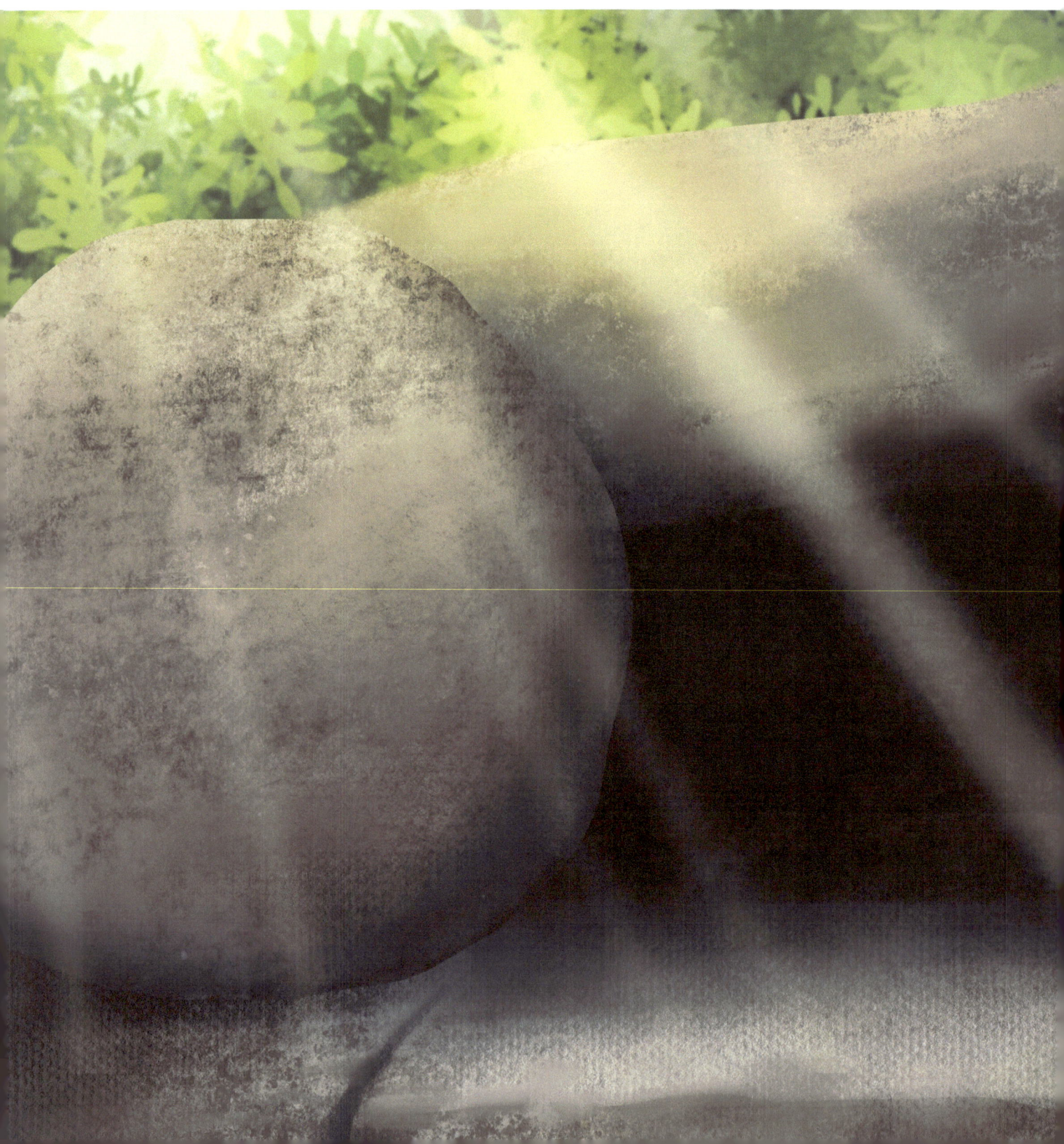

Because of Jesus and his atonement, we can be resurrected like he was. This means, our bodies and spirits will come back together one day after we die.

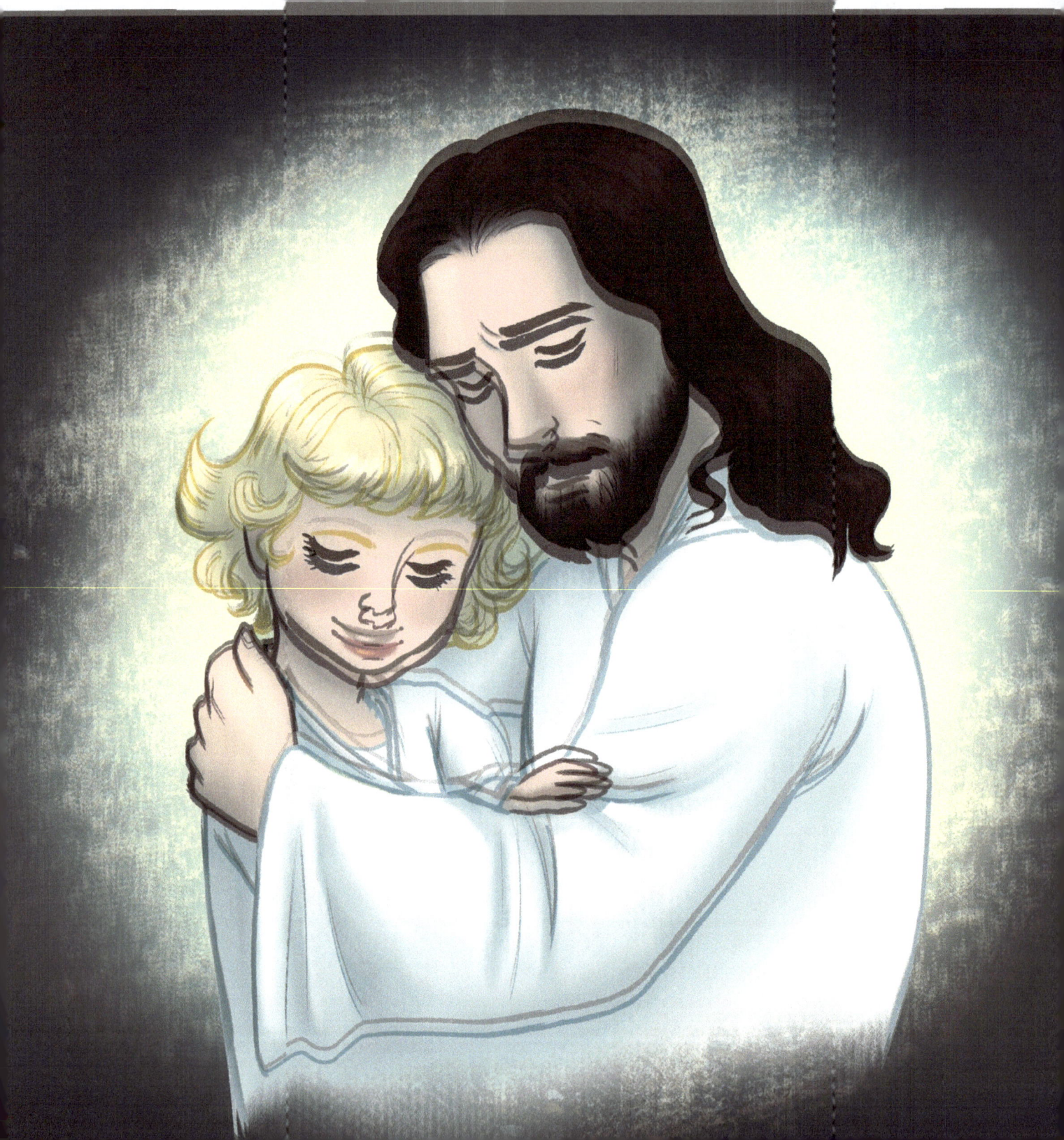

When we are resurrected we can live with Heavenly Father and Jesus again.

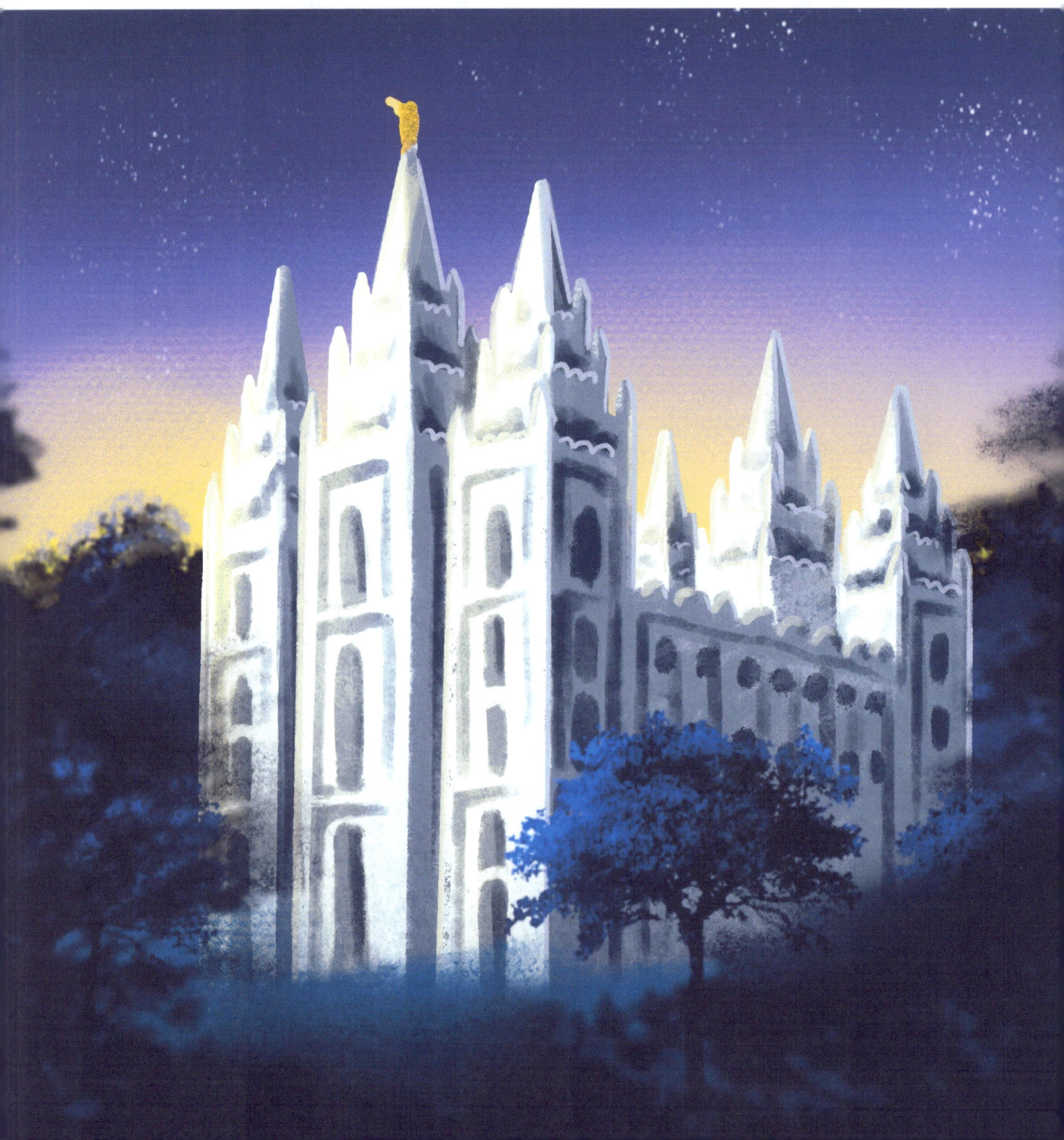

Heavenly Father loves us very much! He gave us this great plan so we can return to Him.

The End.

DISCLAIMER:
This book is not affiliated with the
Church of Jesus Christ of Latter Day Saints.

www.ingramcontent.com/pod-product-compliance
Lightning Source LLC
Chambersburg PA
CBHW051925210526
45473CB00006B/2133